Armand de Potter

The Egyptian Pantheon

Armand de Potter

The Egyptian Pantheon

ISBN/EAN: 9783337240011

Printed in Europe, USA, Canada, Australia, Japan

Cover: Foto ©ninafisch / pixelio.de

More available books at **www.hansebooks.com**

— THE —

EGYPTIAN PANTHEON.

An Explanatory Catalogue

—: OF :—

EGYPTIAN ANTIQUITIES,

Collected and classified with especial reference to the religion and funerary rites of Ancient Egypt, by

ARMAND DE POTTER,

And exhibited in the Egyptian section of the archæological department in the

Anthropological Building,

WORLD'S COLUMBIAN EXPOSITION,

Chicago, U. S. A.

ARMAND DE POTTER, PUBLISHER,
1122 Broadway, New York.

PRICE 35 CENTS.

IMHOTEP.

THE

EGYPTIAN PANTHEON.

An Explanatory Catalogue

— OF —

EGYPTIAN ANTIQUITIES.

COLLECTED AND CLASSIFIED WITH ESPECIAL REFERENCE TO THE RELIGION AND FUNERARY RITES OF ANCIENT EGYPT.

— BY —

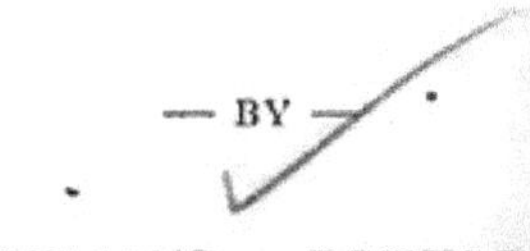

ARMAND DE POTTER

Member of the American Oriental Society; Member of the Archæological Society of France, etc.

CONTENTS:

Introduction.

THESE little monuments, for the greater part from 18 to 40 centuries old, take us back to the oldest known civilization, teaching us its religion and art—therefore, no other monuments, whether large or small, have greater interest attaching to them.

This collection, with its catalogue, is the result of the research and careful selection of an amateur American archæologist, Orientalist and traveller; it is comparatively small, and perhaps incomplete, but made without the aid of any government or association, and, it is hoped, will prove of interest in our great Columbian Exposition. As this is only intended as a catalogue, but few brief notes are given, yet some remarks on the History of Egypt, her Mythology and Funerary Rites will, it is believed, not be out of place.

ARMAND DE POTTER.

Brief Sketch of Egyptian History. *

The known history of Egypt begins with the foundation of what is called the "Ancient Empire," about 5,000 years before our era. It lasted up to the 9th Dynasty, a period of 1940 years. Menes was the first king. Monuments of the first three dynasties show the archaic Egyptian period of art.

With the 4th Dynasty (4235 B. C.) began a period of progress in art, and many monuments yet extant date from that time—among them, the *Pyramid of Cheops*, the Pyramid of Chefren, and the exquisitely cut statue of that king, in the Ghizeh Museum, are also of this Dynasty. At the end of the 5th Dynasty, 5600 years ago, when now civilized and polished Europe was still in a state of savage life—when classic Greece and artistic Italy were unknown—the banks of the Nile were lined with cities that attested a high state of civilization, a powerful monarchy; wealth, commerce, arts; and a people both wise and polished. Then followed a period of some 300 years during which history is obscure. With the 9th Dynasty (3358 B. C.) began the "Middle Empire," which lasted until 1703 B. C.—Everything was transformed to some extent, and the monuments of this period show that it was the Renaissance of Egypt—at first rude and imperfect; then, showing that the conceptions and skill which had produced marvels five centuries before, were still alive in the Nile Land.

In 3064 B. C., the 12th Dynasty had Osertassen and later

---

* *From de Potter's Practical Guide to the Orient.*

Amenemha—both powerful monarchs, and with them Egypt seems to have risen again to her ancient glory in learning, art and conquests. The Tombs of Beni-Hassan show to what height art had risen during this Dynasty.

Egypt continued in prosperity until the 14th Dynasty (about 2400 B.C.), when suddenly, the whole land was overrun by the Hyksos, and during four centuries, the so-called "Shepherd Kings" ruled over Eygpt. But while the Hyksos ruled by military strength—the Egyptians ruled their conquerors through religion and learning.

The "New Empire" began with the 18th Dynasty (1703 B. C.) and ended in about 340 B. C. During the first years of the 18th Dynasty, commerce grew, magnificent temples and palaces were built—and Eygpt reached a state of prosperity hitherto unknown. One of the first and greatest kings of this Dynasty was Amosis, who rebuilt many of the old temples. He was succeeded by Amenophis. Then came Thothmes I., who led his conquering army into Ethiopia, to the South; the land of Canaan and Palestine, to the East and North; and as far as the Euphrates. Later, his son Thothmes III., still a boy, became king—but under the regency of an Egyptian Catherine whose name was Hatasoo, and who ruled during 17 years. She left some of the finest monuments in Egypt—and made some of the boldest expeditions, her armies always returning victorious. Her magnificent obelisk in red granite, still *in situ*, amid the stupendous ruins of Karnak, was quarried, carved, polished and placed in position in the short time of five months. The walls of her cenotaph-temple at Deir-el-Bahari are covered with remarkable bas-reliefs, depicting her expedition to the land of Punt, and her return by boat—the whole showing what the Egyptian army and navy were like, some 4000 years ago. Upon the death of this interesting woman, her brother, Thothmes

III., took the power in his own hands and ruled with great wisdom and firmness. He left countless monuments to attest a peaceful, prosperous and glorious reign of 47 years. During this period, Egypt controlled the countries about her. His successors maintained this vast power in a peaceful manner. Amenhotep III. added to the temple of Karnak and built the temple of Luxor, also a great temple across the river, at the entrance of which stood the two "Singing Memnon," (about 1600 B. C.), now all there is left of a vast monument which stood in the midst of the splendid "city with the hundred gates."

At this time Thebes was at the zenith of her glory and many of her palace-temples were then erected or rebuilt.

With Rameses I. began the 19th Dynasty (1462 B. C.) About this time Egypt lost some of her distant provinces and was continually threatened by warlike nations—but Sethi I. reconquered and ruled over Punt, Syria and Armenia. To him we owe the great Hypostyle Hall at Karnak, one of the most wonderful architectural monuments of antiquity; also, the temple of Abydos. His successor, Rameses II., reigned 67 years. Like Thothmes III., we find him a great builder, and his name appears upon hundreds of monuments. The poem of Pentaour on the walls of Karnak relates his heroism during a war with the Khetas. Many inscriptions refer to him as a hero and a great captain. It is supposed to have been under him that the Jews worked on canals and made brick, and it is under his successor, Meneptah, that they left Egypt.

The 20th Dynasty (1288 B. C.) began with Rameses III., to whose glory the temple of Medinet Aboo was built. Toward the end of this Dynasty, the priests conspired against the Pharaohs and at last the crown of Egypt was placed upon the head of the high priest. This seems to have been the beginning of Egypt's decadence, caused by internal division and civil strife. In 1100 B. C., Egypt is divided into several kingdoms, losing all preponderance abroad—while on the other hand, Asiatic influence is felt on the banks of the Nile. Yet, a hundred years later, during a short period of reaction, Sheshak leads an army into Palestine, takes Jerusalem and forces the Jews to pay tribute. It was soon after this that the capital was transferred to the delta, and later, during the 26th Dynasty (about 665 B. C.), art again reached almost perfection. This time is known as the Saitic Epoch, and to it belong some of the finest monuments found in Egypt.

In 527 B. C., all Egypt was ruined by Cambyses, and became a mere province of Persia. This lasted for 121 years, when Egypt freed herself, but only to be reconquered; and at last, during the 31st Dynasty (332 B. C.), the great captain, Alexander, founded the Macedonian Dynasty; being succeeded by the Ptolemies, who gave Egypt an era of peace, lasting 275 years, known as the Greek or 33d Dynasty.

Many monuments were restored, and some beautiful temples erected—among them Denderah, Edfou, Esneh. It was one of the Ptolemies who brought back some 25,000 statues from Persia. They established a museum, several schools of learning, the library at Alexandria with 400,000 volumes.

Like Carthage, Central Europe, Greece and Syria,—Egypt at last fell in the hands of the Romans.

The 34th Dynasty (from 30 B. C.) is that of the Roman Emperors. Under their control, the ancient capitals went to ruin and Alexandria became a mere provincial capital.

But in 364 A. D., the Roman Empire itself being dismembered, Egypt became a province of the Empire of the East. In 381 A. D., Theodosius decreed the closing of all pagan temples and the destruction of all monuments, statues and sculptures of divinities It is estimated that some

40,000 statues were destroyed, and nearly all the temples, more or less—leaving only ruins of the former splendor of 50 centuries. From that time, the Egyptians were known as Copts, and Christianity was the official religion until 640 A. D., when Islam invaded Egypt and built a mosque in Cairo, just 18 years after the Higira.

The Pantheon—Principal Divinities.

The religion of the Egyptians seems to have been based on the idea of one God, to whom they gave many attributes and characters; symbolized oftentimes by animals which were regarded as sacred by the people, who were unable to look beyond the symbol and demanded something visible—something to bring the divinities nearer and make them tangible; thence the seeming worship of animals.

They, no doubt, knew that kneeling before a white cow, they were not praying to Isis—but to a representation.

Every city had its favorite divinity, or rather triad, consisting of the god, wife and son; as for example, at Memphis, Ptah, Sekhet and Imhotep.

Ptah (See No. 11), having preceeded Ammon, represented chaos or night, as Ammon does the sun or day. Ptah is referred to as "the sculptor, the artist, who in his character of potter, turned on his wheel, the egg from which the world sprang forth"—"he who forged the iron vault of heaven and cast the golden-winged scarabæus"—"the architect of the world," etc. He was believed to be incarnate in the *sacred bull*, and as such worshipped in Memphis (see No. 23). As the midday sun he became Ra and was called "the father of Ra"—as the setting sun he became Osiris, therefore often represented as a mummified god, and then called Ptah-Sokar (see No. 11). He was the supreme divinity at Memphis, and chief of the triad, composed of himself, Sekhet (see No. 12) and their son Imhotep (see No. 21).

Ptah is usually represented in the form of a mummy, holding a *sceptre* with the *ankh* or ansated cross, and the tat; on his head he wears a tight-fitting cap.

Ra (see No. 118) was the midday sun—the luminary force, the infinite, incomprehensible combination of divine spirit.

Ra was believed to make himself visible through the sun, while he became invisible and mysterious as Ammon Ra, is represented as a man with a hawk's head, surmounted by the sun-disk and asp.

Ammon-Ra (see No. 10). Ammon was to the Egyptians what Zeus was to the Greeks or Jupiter to the Romans. He was called "the king of gods, power of powers." He was chief of the triad worshipped at *Thebes*, and composed of himself; his wife Mout or Nut, who personifies the sky, and is often referred to as "the mother of the gods;" their son, Khons (see No. 20); Mout or Nut, and Khons, being in reality but other names for Isis and Horus, but with different attributes. The *ram* was sacred to Ammon-Ra.

Ammon-Ra is usually represented erect; he wears on his head, the *red crown* of Lower Egypt with two feathers, representing the north and south.

A triad worshipped more or less all over Egypt, with a few changes, according to localities, was composed of Osiris, Isis and Horus:—

Osiris (see No. 1), representing the setting sun, "the rise and fall of the Nile, the decay of all things on earth" and at the same time, the everlasting renewal of life. During his life on earth, Osiris spread civilization and the influence of good everywhere (see No. 22), and was murdered by his brother *Set*, the god of evil. His body was cut into fourteen pieces and scattered, but collected by Isis with the assistance of her sister *Nephthys*. They had the body embalmed and enterred according to the rules prescribed in the *Book of the Dead* under the supervision of *Anubis* and *Thoth*. The embalming and burial of Osiris served as a model for all others, and the usual name given to the dead is also Osiris.

The tomb of Osiris is supposed to have been at Abydos. Osiris is especially represented as the God and Judge of the dead, whom he resurrects. He is always represented in human form, but as a mummy, with his hands uncovered, holding the crook or sceptre and the scourge, emblems of sovereignty; on his head, he wears the crown of Upper Egypt, generally ornamented at the sides with ostrich feathers, symbol of truth.

Isis (see No. 7), "sister and wife of Osiris," the Mother of Horus, seems to have surpassed all the gods in the Pantheon of the Egyptians, and was worshipped above all other divinities. She was called "the good goddess," and represented primordial nature. She is often referred to as "mistress of and governing all the elements;" "representing alone all the gods and goddesses." She is said to have referred to herself as "that which has been and always will be"—and again, "without me, there is nothing." The worship or mysteries of Isis are said to have had a great moral influence over the life of women. She was also the goddess of health and as such, invoked by the sick. She was the chief divinity at Philæ, where she had a beautiful temple still extant—but she was also worshipped in nearly all the temples of Egypt. A white cow was the animal sacred to Isis. As mother of man, she was called *Hathor* (see No. 26 B); as wife of Ammon, she was *Mout* or *Nut*; as goddess of wisdom, she was called *Neith* (see No. 23 B), and appeared under different names and with different attributes in all the triads.

While Isis was still alone in the universe, *Apap*, (see No. 37 and 224), the serpent (evil), came to counteract her good influence, but she conquered the monster. She became the wife of her brother, Osiris, whom after his death she resuscitated as Horus, (see below)—the whole myth symbolizing good overcoming evil and the resurrection of the dead.

Isis is often represented nursing Horus, and generally with a disk and horns, these referring to her being the mother of Horus, the rising sun. Sometimes, her head is surmounted by the vulture, emblem of maternity.

Horus, (see No. 9, 19), representing the rising sun, was called the son of the great goddess," "the avenger of his father," "the living good." He was the chief divinity at Edfou, the Appolinopolis of the Greeks. The hawk was the animal sacred to Horus (See No. 25). He conquered Set, the destroyer of his father, but under the divine influence of Isis.

Horus is often represented as a man with the hawk's head, surmounted by the *pschent*; sometimes as a youth (see No. 19), and again, simply as a hawk.

Besides the above, among the principal local triads, were Ra, Khons-Lunus and Pasht; Horus, Isis and Nephthys; Thoth, as the moon, Mout or Nut, the sky, and Ma, as daughter of the sun.

The triads were often changed by the introduction of other divinities. Among favorite divinities found to have been one of a triad, or to have been the principal divinity in some temple—were *Hathor, Nofer-Hotep, Bes, Set or Typhon, Neith, Nofer-Tum, Sebek, Ptah-Embryo, Aah or Lunus, Anubis.*

These are referred to further in the catalogue. But this brief sketch of a subject on which volumes have been written, would be incomplete without a special reference to **Thoth**, the scribe of the gods and founder of religion. He represented wisdom and learning in general; was called "recorder of Osiris," as judge of the dead; also "messenger of the gods;" and "god of the new moon," with the name of Thoth Lunus. He is often referred to as "the inventor of language, the divine intelligence, the living word, the divine food." His writings are said to have numbered 35,000 volumes, including rules for the entire system of worship and almost all sciences. Thoth says, "no thought of ours can conceive God, nor can language define Him. That which is incorporeal, invisible, without form, cannot be grasped by our senses; that which is eternal cannot be measured by a rule of time. God, the immutable truth, cannot be understood on earth. We can only come to this truth and uplift the veil—by the destruction of the corporeal organs—the spirit, which does not die, being enlightened." While Thoth made rules for worship, he also foretold its confusion: "Oh, Egypt, he says, a time will come when instead of having a pure religion and worship, thou shalt only have ridiculous fables, incredible to posterity—and only words engraved on stone will endure to attest thy real piety. Thoth, whoever he may have been, priest or prophet, foresaw the future of Egypt, when the divinity would be not only multiplied, but represented by living animals, and further by numberless *amulets* as symbols of divine attributes. The *Ibis* (see 33, 45), and the *Cynocephalus* (see 36), were both sacred to Thoth.

Thoth is generally represented with the head of an *ibis*, holding a pen and tablet, or simply as an ibis.

N. B.—Names given above in *italics* will be found explained in the catalogue, or in the Glossary (page 35.)

THE CATALOGUE.

N B.—Objects of special excellence for workmanship and color are distinguished by an asterisk *,—those that are both of extra fine workmanship and of value for preservation and rarity, by two * *.

All names or words not explained under the catalogue number will (if printed in *italics*) be found in the little glossary on page 35.

Principal Divinities.

Statuettes in bronze and other objects, several of which are mounted on base of Egyptian alabaster

1. ***Osiris**—(see p. 8), as a mummy, wearing the crown of Upper Egypt; in front the *uræus*, emblem of divinity; holds the *crook* or *sceptre* and *scourge*, emblems of sovereign power.

2. ***Osiris**—Same as No. 1, but with the *ostrich* feather, emblem of truth, on either side of the crown. The necklace is chiseled around the shoulders; inscription on base.

3. ****Osiris**—Same as No. 2, but feathers and necklace chiseled and incrusted with gold. Saitic epoch.

4 and 5. **Osiris**—On the back is **Isis**, with the horns of a

cow, as mother, and with wings spread, protecting the mummy of Osiris.

6. **Osiris** sitting.

7. **Isis** and **Horus**—See p. 10.

7b. **Isis**—see p. 9.

8. **Isis**, wearing the *Klaft*, the royal headdress, surmounted by a *throne*; which is the hieroglyph for her name. It also stands for the word *house*. In this connection, it is interesting to know that Hathor means house of Horus.

9. **Horus** (see p. 10), with the head of a sparrow-hawk, surmounted by the *pschent*, emblem of rule over the North and South, or Upper and Lower Egypt—being a combination of the white crown of Upper Egypt and the red crown of Lower Egypt. The sparrow-hawk was sacred to Horus; he is generally represented as a man with the hawk's head, and holding the *ankh*, emblem of life. See also No. 19.

10. ***Ammon-Ra** (see p. 8) wears the shenti, sort of apron, and as head-dress, the red crown of Lower Egypt, surmounted by the sun-disk, and two feathers, representing the North and South.

11. ***Ptah-Sokar**, (see 7), represented in the shape of a mummy with a close fitting cap on the head; wears a necklace and holds the *tat*, emblem of stability, the *ankh* and the *user*, emblems of serenity or sovereign power. See also 12, 21, 23. Saitic epoch.

12. ****Pasht**, a form of Sekhet, (see No. 63), wife or "favorite of Ptah;" represented with a cat's head; holds a *lotus* blossom. (See No. 39). She is often referred to as the enemy of *Set*, (Typhon), and says of herself, "I set a fiery blaze of millions between Osiris and his enemy, diverting all evil from him and keeping his enemies aloof." These words almost prove that Pasht or Sekhet is but another name for Isis.

The cat was sacred to Pasht. She had temples at Karnak. Bubastis and other places.

13, 14, 15. Pasht sitting.

16. Sebek, with the head of a *crocodile*; has the *pschent* for head-dress; holds the *ankh* in the right hand and a sceptre in the left. He is called the companion of Set, yet whose evil influence he counteracts. By some scholars he is supposed to be a sun-god—no doubt, Horus, under a different name and attributes. The *crocodile* was sacred to him. He was the chief divinity at Ombas in Upper Egypt, and was also worshipped in other places, See Nos. 35 and 117.

17. Harpocrates, pointing his finger to his mouth; under the Greek influence worshipped as the god of silence. It is probable that this represents Horus as a child—the expression of eternal youth, the daily renewal of all life, through the rising sun.

18. Khons-Lunus or *Aah*, as a mummy, holding a *sceptre* and *flagellum*; the "lock of youth" hangs over his right shoulder; above the forehead is the *uræus*, surmounted by the crescent and disk. Khons-Lunus is the same as Khons, but with a different attribute, and as such belongs to the Thebeian *triad*. He is the representative god of rejuvenescence. See also 20.

19. Horus, as a child. The "*Lock of Youth*" hangs over his right shoulder; wears the *klaft*; in front, the *uræus*, surmounted by a head-dress composed of the *uræus* and two *ram's horns*, emblem of sovereignty and the heat of the sun. This is sometimes taken for a form of Ammon-Ra.

20. Khons, the rising sun, sometimes called Khons-Lunus; wears the *klaft* with *uræus*, surmounted by the crescent and disk. (See also 18.)

21. **Imhotep (see p. 8). He is represented with a ong dress and holds an open scroll of papyrus on his knees;

his head is covered by a close-fitting cap; his eyebrows and lids are encrusted with gold. *Saitic epoch.* He was the "eldest son of Ptah," the god of medicine, called Esculapius by the Greeks; one of the triad of Memphis, and was worshipped there in a temple called the "Asklepieon" by the Greeks. The sick came to his temple from distant provinces, and many were cured of chronic diseases. In such a case, they left a votive offering, generally representing such a member of the body as had been diseased, or a statuette of the god.

22. ****Nofer-Hotep,** wears the *schenti;* on head a whig, above the *pschent;* carries a long staff or *sceptre.* This magnificent statuette of the *saitic epoch,* represents Nofer-Hotep, a personification of Osiris, in the act of carrying civilization throughout the world.

23. ****Apis,** the sacred bull with the *uræus*, and certain spots indicative of the divine incarnation of Ptah in him. The triangle on his forehead is incrusted with gold, (see Ptah p. 7.) The sacred bull was considered the second life and personification of Ptah, and as such worshipped at Memphis. He had a beautiful stable connected with his temple, and there, was visited by thousands of worshippers. Upon his death, all the land was in mourning, his body was embalmed with care, enclosed in a magnificent granite sarcophagus, and deposited in the *Serapeum.* The mourning and lamentation lasted until a successor, bearing certain special marks, had been found; among these was, first of all, a white triangle on his forehead, then on his back an eagle, on his right side a crescent, and under his tongue a lump in the shape of a *scarabæus.*

24. **Apis.**

25. **Hawk,** sacred to Horus. The head is surmounted

by the *pschent*, the crown which Horus placed upon his head, thereby uniting the north and south.

23 B., **24** B., **25** B.—**Neith,** (see p. 10,) represented with crown of Lower Egypt. Neith was but another name for Isis; she was the Minerva of the Egyptians, and chiefly worshipped at Sais. She was also the personification of the space in which the sun moves. Plutarch quotes an inscription on the statue of this goddess at Sais—"I am the Universe, the Past, the Present and the Future, no mortal has ever raised the vail which surrounds me."

26 B. **Hathor,** Isis represented as the divine mother, her name signifying house of Horus (see No. 8). hence mother of the rising sun, is often represented as a cow, expressing the idea of motherhood· Hathor, like Neith and Mout, personifies the celestial space in which the sun moves, and of which Horus is the personification as the rising sun. The finest temple dedicated to her was at Denderah, but she was worshipped throughout Egypt.

26. **Bronze pales or libation vases,** one being especially well preserved with reliefs representing myths. These vases were often suspended in tombs for the goddess of heaven to pour out a regenerating drink to the dead.

27. **Set,** represented with a bunch of feathers for head-dress; was the god of evil who killed Osiris. (See p. 9.)

28. **Pallacide,** in prayer.

29. **Sceptre-head,** surmounted by the *atew*, representing *Khnum-Ra*, another name for Ammon; favorite divinity in Nubia, and worshipped on the island of Elephantine. He was called "the maker of gods and men." (See No. 75).

30. **Cat,** sacred to Pasht. (See No. 12).

31. **Urœus,** (Harpollon,) divine and royal symbol, emblem of supreme power, found on head-dress of gods and kings.

32. Crouching ox.

33. **Ibis**, sacred to Thoth. (See p. 11.)

34. **Sphinx**, with a branch running from the back; use unknown. The Sphinx is said to represent the god Horus, the rising sun; but most writers differ as to the symbolization, except on the theory that the body of the lion united to the head of a man symbolized strength combined with intelligence, which is accepted by many.

35. **Crocodile**, sacred to Sebek, (see No. 16.). Sometimes the Crocodile alone represented the dark regions.

36. **Cynocephalus**, a sort of monkey sacred to Thoth. In the judgment of the soul, often illustrated in tombs, he is seen sitting on the handle of the scales, giving equilibrium of which he was the symbol.

37. **Asp** or serpent **Apap**, representing darkness and evil, which was overcome by light (the sun) and good, represented by Horus or Ra; was also tamed by Isis, the good goddess.

38. **Latus**, a fish sacred to Hathor and Khnum-Ra, and worshipped at Latopolis (Esneh).

39. **Lotus**, emblem of the daily reappearance of the sun, and especially of the resurrection. It is found on the head of Nofer-Tum (see No. 48,) and Horus is sometimes seen from its calyx.

40. Sacrificial table, with a priest kneeling, and a *frog*, the symbol of the resurrection of the dead.

41 and **42.** Shields or ægis, surmounted by the heads of divinities, probably Sekhet and Imhotep.

43. Serpent, with woman's head.

44. Handle of a priest's magic rod, the "our-hekaou," ending in a hawk's head.

45. **Ibis**—See No. 33.

46. **Shou**, represented kneeling with arms raised, upholding the heavens. He represented the space between heaven and earth; was the son of Ra, and he separated the heavens from the earth.

47. ***Imhotep**, a head—see No. 21. *Saitic epoch.*

48. **Nofer-Tum**, with head surmounted by a *lotus*. He was the son of Ptah and Sekhet—a primordial divinity; like Horus representing the rising sun; often called "the protector of the two worlds." *Saitic epoch.*

49. **Isis**, head surmounted by the disk between the horns of a cow. See Nos. 7 to 8 and p. 9.

50. **Osiris**—see No. 1 and p. 8.

51. Handle of a priest's rod.

52. Handle of **Sistrum**, with Hathor head. The *sistrum* was used in religious festivals by the *pallacides*. Representations of sistrums in enameled porcelain, often with Hathor head, were deposited in the tombs after having been broken in sign of mourning, (see Nos. 145 and 146. The sistrum for actual use consisted of a bronze oval hoop, with a handle, little movable bars being inserted in the hoop.

53. Twelve **Amulets** and divinities in bronze.

54 to 61. For these numbers, see p. 32.

Divinities and Amulets in Enameled Stone Porcelain and Fayence.

Small statuettes of divinities and amulets were produced by thousands, and many were of very fine workmanship. They were made of various semi-precious stones, of porcelain, limestone or fayence—the latter being rarely of ordinary clay, but pulverized limestone, and nearly always covered with enamel in green, yellow, red, brown, violet and blue; the first named being the favorite color of the most ancient dynasties, while objects in a deep blue enamel are among the rarest found. Those used for amulets were generally fastened to a necklace and worn around the neck, and, after, death buried with the mummy, as were in fact all such objects, including jewels. The amulets represented divinities, sacred animals and religious emblems of all sorts—some remaining still unexplained.

62. ***Anubis**, represented with the head of a jackal Anubis (Anepou), son of Nephthys, was the chief divinity of several *nomes* in Upper Egypt. He was believed to preside at funerals and was called "the master of the enemies," "conqueror of the enemies of his father Osiris," showing here again that Anubis is but another name for Horus.

63. ***Sekhet**, seated on a throne is represented with the head of a lioness, and holding a sistrum. See No. 12.

64. **Lunus**, or Aah, with sceptre.

65. **Ammon-Ra.**

66. **Kohns-Lunus**, with hawk's head, surmounted by the crescent and disk.

67. Cynocephalus—see No. 36.

68. ***Ptah-Embryo**, represented as a deformed dwarf, between Isis and Nephthys; stands on two *crocodiles* and presses two serpents against his breast; on his shoulders are two *hawks*; on his head, a *scarabæus*; on his back a winged Isis.

69. **Ptah-Embryo** in green enameled limestone.

70. **Set** or Typhon, cut in *pietra-dura*. See No. 27.

71. **Ptah-Sokar**—see No. 11

72. **Hapi**, with the head of a monkey, one of the four genii, considered protectors of the intestines of the dead. See p. 28.

73. **Anubis**—see No. 62.

74. Ptah-Embryo.

75. **Khnum-Ra,** represented as a man with the head of a ram. See No. 29.

76. **Thoueris,** represented as a hippopotamus; the wife of Set and protectress of women in pregnancy. She had a special sanctuary at Karnak.

77. **Ammon-Ra**—see p. 8.

78. A priest playing the flute.

80. **Anubis**—see 62.

81. **Thoueris**—see 76.

82 and **83**. **Ammon-Ra**—see p. 8.

84. Ptah-Sokar—see 11.

85. Hapi—see 72.

86. Anubis—see 62.

87 and **88**. **Bes**, a grotesque dwarf with a head-dress of feathers; was the god of mirth. He was believed to preside over childbirth—therefore, often represented in the *mammisi*.

89. **Sekhet**, or a lotus colonnette.

90. **Sekhet**, sitting.

91. Monkey or cynocephalus.

93. Cat, sacred to Pasht.

94 **Ammon-Ra** with ram's head, wings and sun-disk. See p. 8.

95. Ammon-Ra.

96. Anubis—see 62.

97. **Horus** as a child—see 19.

98. **Isis,** nursing Horus—see p. 10.

99. *Ammon-Ra with ram's head—see p. 8.

100. Sekhet—see 12.

101. Thoueris—see 76.

102. Hathor—see 26 B.

104 and **105** B. Shou—see 46.

105. Imhotep—see 21.

106. Lioness, sacred to Sekhet.

107. **Cynocephalus (see 36), holding the *mystic eye*, emblem of the full moon, an amulet worn to ward off all sorts of evil, the effects of the evil eye, also the bites of reptiles. Green-bluish *pietra-dura*.

108. *Cynocephalus in Egyptian alabaster.

109. ***Sacred Hawk** in jade.

110. Same in lapis lazuli.

111. Same in limestone.

112. Cynocephalus.

113. **Ram**, sacred to Ammon-Ra.

114. Same in light green enameled limestone.

115. **Ibis** in green enameled fayence.

116. **Asp**.

117. *Crocodile in green fayence.

118. ***Ra**, with the hawk's head—see p. 8.

119. ***Isis**, in lapis lazuli.

120. ***Khons-Lunus**, with crescent and disk.

121. *Cat, in lapis lazuli.

122. ***Ma**, generally represented with the "feather of truth" on her head; goddess of truth; she introduced the dead in the hall of judgment, before Osiris. In jade.

123. ***Tiaumautew**, with the head of a *jackal* and prayer on obverse; small stele-shape green fayence, represents one of the protectors of the intestines. (See p. 28.)

124. Head in green enameled porcelain.

125. Eye in marble, from mummy. (See p. 30.)

126. **Hathor-head**, in blue enameled porcelain.

127. **Set**, with *cartouche* on obverse.

128. Two head-rests, in onyx. These little amulets were placed in the sarcophagus with the dead, helping to assure peaceful rest in the other world.

129. Hare, with *cartouche*. The hare was sacred to the goddess Unit, a secondary divinity of the Greek epoch.

130. **Nofer-Tum**, head surmounted with lotus and feathers, and his mother Sekhet, represented as a lioness.

130b. **Horus**, between Isis with a throne and Nephthys with a sort of tower on the head.

Amulets and other objects found in tombs.

131. Four *mystic eyes* tied together by a *lotus*.

132. **Mystic eye in blue enamel fayence.

133. Same.

134. **Colonnette** in feldspar. These little amulets, ending in a lotus flower, are generally in feldspar or green porcelain. They represent green, fresh vegetation, the daily renewal of nature, and are the symbol of continued life and prosperity.

135. Colonnette in porcelain.

136. **Ring** in fayence.

137. Lotus flower.

138. Mummy heart in stone.

139. Seal in wood.

141. 142. 143. 144. ***The Tat**, sometimes called the Nile Key; is the emblem of stability. Also referred to as "the spine of Osiris."

145. *Sistrum handle with Hathor-head; in bluish-green enameled porcelain.

146. Same, surmounted by a *naos*, with Hathor-head; brown porcelain.

147. *Handle in fayence, with gilded *cartouche* of Amasis, 26th Dynasty.

148. **Bes.**

149-153 c. For these numbers, see collection of scarabæi, below, on this page.

154-159 c. (See p. 24.)

160-176. (See p. 32.)

177-193. ***Collection of Amulets**, including 95 choice objects, mainly in *pietra-dura*, semi-precious stones, and a few in enameled porcelain of fine color and finish.

180. Frog, emblem of resurrection; in lapis lazuli.

181. Frog in jade.

182. *Curious amulet, representing the mystic eye, surmounted by a crouching lioness, upon three small eyes.

183. Head rest in onyx.

184. Colonnette in bloodstone.

185. Same, in lapis lazuli.

186. **Horus** between Isis and Nephthys.

187. **Sistrum**, in blue enameled porcelain.

188. **Ra**, in fine green enameled porcelain.

189. **Isis**, head surmounted by a throne.

190. **Urœus**, in blue enameled porcelain.

191. **Anhk**, or *ansated cross.*

192. Two *ostrich feathers*.

193. **Mystic eye** in lapis lazuli.

149-153 C. **Collection of Scarabæi.** Of all amulets, the *scarabæus* generally known as "scarab," was probably the most important. It represents the golden-winged Nile beetle (see x), which at certain seasons disappears in the mud, and suddenly reappears in greatly increased numbers. It was to the Egyptians, first of all, the symbol of creative power; stands as the equivalent of the Egyptian word Kheper, *to become*; was also the symbol of resurrection—the negation of death. Scarabæi are in enameled limestone, fayence and porcelain; also in lapis-lazuli, jade, amethyst, and other precious stones; also, often found in silver and gold. They usually were worn in rings and on necklaces. Large scarabæi were placed on the mummies, sometimes with a prayer from the Book of the Dead, chap. xxx., to take the place of the heart which was removed and put in one of the *canopes*. The prayer referred to reads as follows: "My heart which came from my mother, my heart necessary to my life on earth, do not rise against me—do not testify against me—do not part from me before the great lord of *Amenti*."

149. *Scarabæus in dark bloodstone.

150. *Same in basalt.

151. *Same.

152. **Same in fine, light-green enameled porcelain, bearing the *cartouche* of Thothmes III., surmounted by two ostrich feathers.

153. *Forty-seven scarabæi in pietra-dura and enameled porcelain, among them several bearing royal cartouches and others interesting symbolical subjects.

153 B. *Scarabæus in basalt, the inscription being an invocation to Khnum.

153 C. Winged-scarabæi which were always used to place on mummies—see No. 230.

Jewels and other Precious Objects.

Jewels, including necklaces, rings, bracelets, etc.; more or less valuable, were worn by all classes and were always buried with the dead.

154. **Small Urn, in serpentine. In front is a gilded *cartouche* of the Princess Ounofris; the cover represents a woman's head with the *Klaft*, also gilded.

155. Ring, blue enameled porcelain.

156. Amethyst amulet with intaglio.

157. Ring in alabaster.

158. Ring with *cartouche* of Thothmes III.

158 B. Ring in ivory.

158 C. Ring in bronze.

159. Two mystic eyes in light-green fayence.

159 B. Ring in blue glass with *cartouche* between two ortrich feathers.

160 to **176.** See p. 32.

177 to **193.** Collection of amulets. See p. 23.

194. Three necklaces of beads and amulets in porcelain.

195. Necklace in porcelain.

196. Same.

197. Necklaces, three of which are in pietra-dura and alabaster.

198. Strings and net of porcelaine beads, used to put around mummies.

199. Miscellaneous amulets.

200. Two necklaces of beads and amulets.

201. *Small parrot in bronzed silver.

202. Seal ring in bronze.

203. *Ring with *scarabæus.*

203 B. Seal ring in silver with a royal personage sitting on a throne.

204. Ear-rings in gold.

205. Ring in wood with *cartouche* seal.

206 and **207.** *Gold rings with scarabæi also in gold.

208. **Necklace in gold; its pendant with butterfly in lapis-lazuli, and little gold flies.

209. Ear-ring in gold with amethyst.

210. Pin in gold.

211. *Necklace in gold with enameled pendant.

212. *Necklace in gold with gold and lapis lazuli beads.

213. Necklace in agate and coral.

214. Ear-ring in gold.

215. *Ring in gold with two divinities (Sekhet and Imhotep), in repoussé.

216. Ring in gold with mystic eye in cornaline.

217. *Ring in gold with *scarabæus*.

218. Ring in gold with aqua-marine stone.

219. *Ear-rings in gold—Ptolemaic epoch.

220. Ring in gold with scarabæus.

221. *Ring in gold with scarabæus in sardonyx.

222. **Thirteen amulets in gold forming necklace. From the royal mummies at Deir-el-Bahari.

223. **Sitting *Scribe* in basalt, partly restored.

224. Serpent coiled, tamed by Isis, whose hands are visible on either side—a rare fragment. This represented Isis taming the serpent Apap, overcoming the evil influence which it had on humanity.

225. Papyrus.

226. *Mummy necklace. These necklaces were made especially for the dead and were placed upon the breast.

Sepulchral Figurines and other objects Relating to the Burial of the Dead.

With regard to the burial of the dead, it will no doubt be quite *apropos* to give here a brief sketch of the manner in which the ancient Egyptians disposed of their dead.

The preservation of human bodies from corruption was the first thing looked for and the Egyptians excelled in the art of embalming. It is well known that they believed in immortality and transmigration of souls—in "the being born again"—but by transmigration into animals, and finally after 3,000 years of rapid wandering, into another man. To this, however, was added the belief that as long as the body was not entirely destroyed the soul could return to it and stay by it—hence, the great care for preventing decay. We learn from Herodotus that "when the death of some person occurred, the women of the house covered their head and face with mud, uncovered their bosom by tying the garments below the waist and went about town screaming and beating themselves; they were joined by all the other women relatives of the deceased." This custom can yet be witnessed in Egypt, parts of Algeria, and in many eastern countries. "After this performance, or preliminary mourning, the body was taken to the place of embalment. Every *necropolis* of Egypt had the houses and working-rooms of the operators—a special priesthood—in its neighborhood. This priesthood was composed of "the chlochytes, the paraschites and the taricheutes." "The enbalmers showed to those who brought the corpse three different models, made of wood and painted so as to imitate a real mummy. The first or most accurate was also the most expensive, and said to be similar to the manner in which Osiris was embalmed. The second class was inferior to the first, in workmanship and cheaper in price; the third, the cheapest of all, was naturally the most inferior in workmanship. Once the selection made and the price fixed, the relatives left the body and the taricheutes began their work—we shall suppose for a first-class embalment:" First, with a bent instrument they extracted through the nostrils as much as they could of the brain, the rest being removed by infusion of drugs. Afterward with a very sharp flint skife they made an incision on the left side of the abdomen in order to extract the intestines. These were immersed in a prepartion of bituminous liquid and deposited in four vases called canopes, except a portion considered unclean and thrown in the river. The canopes were generally in alabaster or limestone and were surmounted by the head of a woman, a hawk, a jackal and cynocephalus—said to represent Nephthys, Horus, Anubis and Thoth—protectors of the intestines and the tomb. Sometimes these differed and were the four genii, also considered protectors—they were Amset, head of a man, guardian of the stomach; Hapi, head of a cynocephalus, small intestines; Tiaumautew, hawk, the heart and lungs; Kebshennow, jackal, the liver. These canopes were placed at the four corners of the sarcophagus; and in cases where all the intestines were thrown into the river, a stone imitation of the canopes was placed, as a symbol, beside the mummy. See No. 257.

"Once the intestines removed, they washed the cavity with palm wine, filling it afterwards with myrrh, cinnamon and other aromatic substances. The corpse was then laid in natron and left in it for seventy days. As soon as this period had elapsed the body was taken out of the natron, washed and bandaged, and finally delivered to the relatives, who put it in a case having the shape of a human body; it was then put in the tomb standing up against the wall." This last statement of Herodotus can hardly be correct as nearly all mummy cases found up to the present were lying on the floor of the tomb.

"The corpses prepared in the second manner had not the left side cut, but injections were made with cedar ointment. The body was then put in the natron, and after seventy days taken out, the entrails coming out macerated. The flesh was also destroyed, only the skin and bones remaining. The third manner of embalmment for the poorer class consisted simply in injecting natron inside the body and macerating the flesh in the natron for the usual period of seventy days."

Diodorus also gives an account which differs in some particulars from the above, but in his we find the usual cost of the two best embalmments:—"One silver talent, about $1200 for the first, and twenty mines, about $400 for the second."

Diodorus gives thirty days instead of seventy as the period of the embalming process, and it is not impossible that Herodotus mistook the full time of mourning with that necessary for embalming. In Genesis L., 2: 3, we read: "And Joseph commanded his servants the physicians to embalm his father—and the physicans embalmed Israel. And *forty days* were fulfilled for him; *for so are fulfilled the days of those which are embalmed*: and the Egyptians mourned for him *three score* and *ten* (70) days."

The fact is that, though sufficiently clear, the accounts of both Herodotus and Diodorus lack, in many respects, in correctness, and much has been learned within the past few years from the mummies themselves, the monuments, tombs and from the reading of papyrus. A great many mummies have been found preserved only with bitumen or asphalt, and although neither of the above mentioned writers referred to this substance in their description, the latter in describing the Lake Asphaltis (Dead Sea), says: "The barbarians carry the asphalt to Egypt and sell it for the embalming of the dead, because not mixing this to the other aromatic substances it would not be possible to obtain the preservation for a long time." Besides being beautifully bandaged, mummies (of the first-class), were decorated in a most expensive manner. Mummies have been found with gilded masks, the head entirely covered with gold leaf, others with the eyes, the mouth and fingers gilded. This work was performed by the colchytes, who received the dried corpses from the taricheutes and bandaged them according to the rite. Necklaces, rings, scarabæi, amulets, rolls of papyrus inscribed with part of the Book of the Dead and sometimes the history of the subject with whom they were buried, were inserted among the bandages, or put with the mummy in the wooden case. **Artificial eyes**, generally enameled, were found in the eye-sockets of many mummies and a large scarabæus was placed in or upon the mummy to take the place of the heart which was removed. See page 24.

Figurines (see No. 158, etc.), of wood, enameled limestone, porcelain or fayence, were always placed in the mummy case, or enclosed in a box like No. 264 and put in the tomb. These figurines are in the shape of an Osiris and usually bear the name of the dead, followed by the phrase, "Illumination of the Osiris X," and chapter VI. from the Book of the Dead, which read as follows: "Oh, respondent here present, may you be reckoned in favor of Osiris X. in place of the offerings not made in the tomb." Then follows a prayer which is addressed, according to Herodotus, "to him whose name should not be uttered," and who was no other than the god Osiris. As every (deceased) Osiris had to work a certain time in the Field of *Amenti*, these figurines were deposited especially to take the place of this work for those who were not accustomed to agricultural labour. On the back of such a figurine is a bag to contain seed, and in the hands the flail and hoe for the labor in the field.

Funeral. As soon as all was ready, the priests were called to the house and the casket carried in solemn procession to the tomb; an altar was erected at the entrance and there with reading of parts from the Book of the Dead it was received into the custody of *Anubis*. Here friends and relatives added such gifts and offerings as were ready and all was deposited together with the mummy and the four canopes in the lower chamber of the tomb.

Among the offerings made were amulets, vases and bottles of water, oil, wine, beer, incense, beef, birds, bread, fruit, corn and wheat; also several articles of furniture. Some of these offerings were repeated on the anniversary of the death. Among the offerings was also a cone in terra-cotta, generally bearing the *cartouche* of the deceased and representing the symbolic bread or food. The Book of the Dead refers to the necessity of 'food' for the journey to *Amenti*—but this 'food' was the sacred science without which no one could pass through all the obstacles met with *en route*. He first was to meet with monsters, servants of Set; crocodiles, serpents and other reptiles—and it is only by possessing a sufficient amount of food—mystic science—that he could overcome the danger. If he gave way to fear, he could not continue his journey; but if he had enough science, he could overcome these monsters and conquer them with a look. At last he won the battle and he exclaimed, "My face is that of the snn, my eyes those of Hathor." Then he met Thoth who handed him a book with further lessons in science necessary to his journey. Arrived on the banks of the infernal river he met a ferryman, sent by Set to lead him astray, but if he possessed enough 'food' (science), he refused, and found the true ferryman, who took him in his boat after having undergone an examination in which he had to give the name with the mystic meaning of each part of the boat and utensils on board. Across the river he landed in the Fields of *Amenti*, where he had to plough, sow and reap. This successfully accomplished, he was conducted before Osiris and his forty-two judges. He had there to defend his life on earth, and, if satisfactory, his heart was weighed against the feather of truth, and sentence was pronounced. Thoth registered it and the soul became an illuminated Osiris, to remain in the spiritual world, and as such is represented as a winged disk, emblem of the rapid flight of the soul, having become a luminary substance. Usually, the details of the funeral, the voyage of the soul to Amenti and before Osiris, are illustrated in sculpture and painting in the tomb.

Sepulchral Figurines and other objects found in tombs.

Sepulchral figurines (see page 30), were manufactured by the thousands, and many have been found in the tombs. Some are of fine workmanship and exquisite color but many are mere pieces of clay, without shape or color. The best are in enameled limestone, porcelain or fayence; also in wood, alabaster, and a few in bronze.

54. ***Sepulchral statuette** in wood. This beautiful statuette shows the *uræus*, emblem of royalty on the forehead; and it bears the *cartouche* of Ramses II.

55. Isis, small statuette in wood.

56. Head of a King in wood.

57. Hawk in wood.

58.
59. } **Sepulchral figurines.**
60.

61. Sepulchral seal in terra-cotta and conical shape. Represented the mystic food (sacred science) for the dead. See page 31.

160. ***Sepulchral figurine** in enameled limestone, representing a mummy, holding the usual agricultural implements, and over the left shoulder a bag to carry seed. For description, see page 30.

161 to **166.** *Same in greenish-blue enameled limestone, each with an inscription.

167 and **168**. Same in light-green enameled fayence.

169 to **170**. Small figurines in fayence but of poor workmanship.

171. Small figurine in fine blue enameled fayence.

172. Four small figurines in fayence of sand and clay.

173. Figurine in wood.

174. Figurine in light-blue fayence.

175 and **176**. Figurines in fayence of sand and clay.

177 to **226**. See p 35.

227. *Figurine in a beautiful deep blue enameled fayence, found with the royal mummies at Deir el-Bahari.

228. *Figurines in deep blue enameled fayence, found with mummies of the prophets of Ammon at Deir-el-Bahari.

229 and **229** B. *Rare figurines found with the mummies of the priests of Ammon at Deir-el-Bahari.

230. **Mummy** of a girl, as found in a tomb at Akhmin. See manner of embalming, etc., page 26.

231. **Mummy of a hawk** in a case of sycamore wood, gilded, with scarabæus on the breast.

232. **Bronze sceptre handle** of a priest of Thoth; lotus flower, surmounted by a cynocephalus.

233. **Winged Scarabæus.**

234. **Cynocephalus** in green fayence.

235. ***Bronze scribe**, sitting on a scarabæus.

236. ***Cup** in blue enameled terra-cotta.

237. **Three Lacrymatories** in Egyptian glass.

238. **Sepulchral amphora,** containing wheat, about 3,000 years old—as found in tomb. See page 31.

239. Sepulchral water-bottle. See page 31

240 and **241**. **Rings**, enameled glass.

242. **Rings** in silver with enamel.

243. **Shou**--see 46.

244. Pig in fayence. The pig is one of the forms under which Set appeared against Horus; was looked upon as the most unclean of animals.

246. Piece of mummy casing.

247. Sepulchral lamp in bronze.

248. Same.

249. Libation Vase.

250. Same.

251. Bronze eye-holders, from mummy. These were used to hold the artificial eyes mentioned on page 30.

252. Head-rest for mummy.

253. Sepulchral statuette in wood.

254. Three sailors from sacred boat, in wood.

255. Winged scarabæi.

256. Collection of sepulchral vases in alabaster.

257. *Canope* in limestone. See p 28.

258. Funerary painting on wood, representing Thoth conducting the dead for judgment before Osiris. See page .

259. Embroideries from tombs at Akhmin—Ptolemaic period.

260. Part of mummy case, painted, representing Nephthys, holding an ostrich feather in each hand—head surmounted by a winged disk, symbol of the sun, progress from East to West, also the rapid flight of the soul.

261. Mask from face of mummy.

262. Mask from inner mummy case, Ptolemaic period.

263. Sepulchral bottle in glass.

264. Box for sepulchral figurines.

265 and **266.** Statuettes in wood.

267. Jackal in wood, sacred to *Anubis*, (see No. 62), is generally seen in tombs, on coffins and on chests for sepulchral figurines.

268. Sepulchral figurines in deep blue enameled fayence.

269. Isis and Horus.

270. The urœus.

Glossary and Index.

Numbers given first refer to No. of object in catalogue.

Numbers given after letter (p) refer to page.

Aah-Lunus, another name for Khons-Lunus, generally represented with a hawk's head, surmounted by the crescent and disk ; sometimes with the 'lock of youth.'

Abydos—the capital of a *nome* ; claimed to possess the tomb of *Osiris*, which made it a holy city and place of pilgrimage. The great temples discovered by Mr. Mariette, are situated on the edge of the desert, some six miles from the banks of the Nile.

Ægis, a sort of shield, usually in bronze in the form of a necklace, called "*ooseck*"—41, 42.

Amenti—journey to, p. 31.

Ammon-Ra, 10, 94, 99 ; p. 8.

Amulets, 53 ; p. 18.

Amset, one of the four sepulchral genii, p. 28.

Ankh or ansated cross, emblem of life—man—creative principle.

Anubis, who presided at funerals, represented as a man with the head of a jackal, or simply as a *jackal* ; 62.

Apap, (asp), symbol of evil and sterility ; 37, 116.

Apis, the bull, sacred to *Ptah* ; 23.

Atew, sacred headdress, the centre being the white miter, emblem of light on either side the *ostrich* feathers ; the *uræus* ; 29.

Bull, see *Apis*.

temples of antiquity, situated on the banks of the Nile, near Luxor.

Klaft, a sort of cap, was a royal headdress.

Lapwing, sacred to *Osiris*.

Lock of Youth, hanging to one side of the head, was the symbol of youth, designated the younger sons of the royal family—also Horus and Khons, 18, 19.

Lioness, sacred to Sekhet, 106.

Lotus : the sun and resurrection, 39.

Lacrymatories, placed in the tomb as an emblem of mourning, 237.

Latus, 38.

Libation pales or vases, 26.

Lunus, see *Aah*.

Ma, goddess of truth' "daughter of the sun," 122.

Mammisi, sort of chapel, often built near a large temple, as at Denderah and Philæ ; called "a chamber of accouchement for the goddess"—was really a place of offering for women *enceinte*.

Masks were placed on mummies' faces in all ages—often they were in gold or gilded pasteboard. Above this was another, making part of the case, generally in cloth or wood, and painted in brilliant colors, p. 29.

Mout or Nut, "mother of the gods," often painted on mummy cases, as the protectress of the dead, was the wife of Ammon. She had the *pschent* for headdress ; sometimes, seen with the *vulture*; wears a long dress and holds the *ankh*.

Mummy, 230.

Mummies—manner of preparing, p. 27.

Mystic eye, 131 to 133 ; 182.

Nephthys, with Isis, protectress of the dead ; "the divine sisters" forming a *triad* with Horus.

Neith, a form of Isis; 23 B.

Nofer-Hotep, a form of Osiris, 22.

Nofer-Tum, the setting sun; 48, 130

Nome, a province.

Ooseck, a large necklace, usually made of beads and semi-precious stones to put on the mummy; 226.

Offerings to the dead, p.

Osiris, 1, 2, 3; p. 8.

Ostrich feather, emblem of truth; 192.

Pallacides, were the priestesses attached to certain rites, especially to the worship or *mysteries of Isis.*

Papyrus was made in crossed layers with the papyrus plant and used for centuries as writing paper in Egypt, 225.

Pasht, wife of *Ptah*; 12.

Philœ, Island of, the most charming spot in Egypt, situated near the First Cataract and celebrated for its beautiful temple of Isis.

Pig, 244.

Priests, always had a great influence upon the government; they had an immense income; were learned in all sciences, each order having a specialty. The high priest was assisted by 18 chief priests, each holding a particular office. The most learned of all was the priest in charge of Thoth's books.

Protectors of the tomb, p. 28.

Pschent, emblematic of rule over the North and South or Upper and Lower Egypt, being a combination of the white crown of Upper and the red crown of Lower Egypt. Horus, it was believed, placed the pschent upon his head, thereby uniting the North and South.

Ptah, chief of the *triad* worshipped at Memphis; 11.

Ptah—Embryo, symbol of transformation; 68.

*Pyramid of Cheops, known also as the "Great Pyramid"

—covers 12 acres of ground with a platform of 40 feet square on its summit and from which there is a magnificient view, embracing the banks of the Nile, several villages and, further away, Cairo, with its palaces, mosques and minarets.

A clever lot of Bedouin-Arabs are always at hand to take the traveler up to the top or inside of the Pyramid.

A long corridor first leads to the Queen's chamber, then up to the King's, or "Chamber of the Sarcophagus," where the sarcophagus of red granite still remains, but the royal mummy was removed long ago, perhaps at the time of an invasion, to some distant tombs for greater security. Other galleries lead higher up to others chambers not now open. All these chambers receive air by narrow passages. There is no longer any doubt that the Pyramids were all built for tombs. As to the age of the Pyramids there are divers opinions, but the great Pyramid was built by Cheops, a king of the IV dynasty (4235 B. C.). We learn from Herodotus that the "Cheops Pyramid" was entirely covered with polished red granite, which was so bright that at his time it was known as the "Pyramid of Light." All this granite and much of the stone has been removed for the building of Cairo. There have been many scientific volumes written on the subject of the great Pyramid, but what difference is it how many cubic inches we find in a corner socket; what does it matter whether or not the Pyramid is the centre of the Universe; whether or not it divinely reveals the system of weights aud measures, as has been claimed lately? Is it not sufficient to behold this stupendous work of 6000 years ago and admire it as one of the wonders of the world without discussing its possible uses? The fact is that many of these theories are published either by cranks or simply to attract the attention of the public, and they do not deserve serious consideration. The great Pyramid, as all the other

Pyramids, *was built for a tomb*, and as such is the most stupendous monument ever erected.

For some reason, as yet unknown, the Egyptians carried the pyramidal shape into all their architectural works, and even to this day we notice that peculiarity in the houses of nearly all villages in Upper Egypt. It is reasonably supposed by some scholars that the word "pyramid" is derived from "piramoye," *i. e.*, sunbeam, and as the sun was the great foundation upon which the whole system of the Egyptian religion rested, I have no doubt but that the Pyramids, as well as the pyramidal shape worked into other monuments, was due to the system of subjecting all art to religious principles and unchangable rules. *

Ra, the Sun, worshipped as the greatest manifestation of divinity, represented as a man with the head of a hawk and sun-disk ; 188.

Ram sacred to Ammon-Ra, was the symbol of the sun's life-giving power ; 113, 144.

Ram's horns, given to Ammon-Ra ; 19.

Red crown, represents Lower Egypt, the North : 23 B.

Religious festivals, were held with magnificent processions around, within and on the roof of the temples. They took place upon the occasion of jubileums, royal coronations, etc.

Sacrifice, table of, 40.

Scarabæus or "scarab," the symbol of immorality, resurrection ; an amulet against sickness, sudden death, etc.; 140 to 153 ; p. 23.

Sceptre, emblem of sovereignty.

Scorpion, sacred to Selk, another name for Isis, as protect-

*From "The Land of the Pharaohs," by Armand de Potter—in "The Old World," Albany, N. Y., February, 1891.

ress of the tomb, represented with a scorpion on the forehead.

Scribe--The sacred scribe beside being priest of Thoth, was the treasurer of all temple or sacerdotal funds ; he was the most learned of all the priests, knowing by heart all of Thoth's sacred writing, including nearly all the known sciences.

Sebek, "the dark regions," Set (Typhon), god of evil ; 27.

Seal-cone, seed *food*.

Serapeum, tombs for the sacred bulls, in the mountains near Sakkarah, discovered by Mr. Mariette ; see Apis, 23.

Shenti, a sort of apron, 10.

Sekhet, 63 ; p. 8.

Sepulchral figurines, p. 30.

Serpent, 43, 224.

Sistrum, 52, 145, 146.

Sphinx, 34.

Shou, represents the earth, kneeling with his arm supholding Mout, the sky ; 46, 104, 105.

Sparrow-Hawk, sacred to Horus.

Sun disk, see *disk*.

Soul—represented by the sun-disk with wings, symbolizing its rapid flight through space. After all its trials and judgment, the soul, it was believed, became a luminary substance. The soul was also represented as a hawk with a human head.

Tat, emblem of stability ; 141 to 144.

Temples—*"The general plan of Egyptian temples is the same. As a rule they are surrounded by an immense wall preceded by a pylon, connected with a second pylon by an avenue of sphinxes. Obelisks or colossal statues of the founder usually stand before the second pylon, which gave access to

a large open court, then to a hall of columns opening into a second hall surrounded with small dark chambers for various religious uses, and connected with the sanctuary. The walls are always covered with hieroglyphics and sculptured reliefs relating to religious rites, conquests, and incidents in the history of Egyptian rulers.

It is supposed that the inner temple was a mystery to the public, and open only to the priests, king, and a few initiated. The great processions that took place in the outer court and on the roof, were witnessed by the people standing below and outside." *

Thebes, the ancient city, "with the hundred gates," was situated on both banks of the nile, near and around the present Luxor.

Thoth, "the divine scribe," the founder of religion and messenger of the gods, is usually represented as a man with an *Ibis* head; p. 11.

Thoth-Lunus: the moon.

Thoueris, 76.

Throne, 8.

Tiaumantew, one of the genii of the tomb; 123.

Tombs—The most beautiful tombs are located along the Nile, at Beni-Hassan, Sakharah, and in the mountains near ancient Thebes. The Egyptian regarded the tomb as the true and permanent home—and its solid walls and columns are usually covered with pictures giving the different trades and incidents of life; and as a rule, a large portrait of the principal occupant.

Typhoon, the Greek name for Set.

Triad, the union of three divinities, usually worshipped in the same place and composed of husband and wife, the

*From "A Trip up the Nile," by Armand de Potter, in the Chautauquan Magazine, December, 1891.

male and female principles, while the son expresses divine rejuvenescence and the continuation of all life ; p. 7.

Uræus, divine and royal emblem : supreme power; 31, 190.

User, a sort of sceptre, emblem of serenity or sovereign power.

Vulture, sacred to Mout or Nut ; symbolic of maternity.

Vulture's wings and disk, see *disk*.

White Crown, Upper Egypt, the south ; 1.

www.ingramcontent.com/pod-product-compliance
Lightning Source LLC
Chambersburg PA
CBHW031804090426
42739CB00008B/1156

* 9 7 8 3 3 3 7 2 4 0 0 1 1 *